MdB
Happy Bday
2019
Love
Regina
& Pete

ITALY

IMAGINE & DISCOVER

HERRON

Contents

Introduction

Italy. The cradle of civilization. Home to the Roman Empire and the Roman Catholic Church. Hundreds of years at the heart of European culture stack comfortably atop millennia of ancient history all set against a backdrop of unfathomable natural beauty.

Sparkling crystal coastline encircles the iconic boot-shaped country, while inland mountain ranges rise to spectacular heights dipping here and there to give way to cool glacial lakes. Hiking, kayaking, and skiiing are all catered for inland, while luxury liners, sailing boats, water sports, swimming, and sun-lounging keep visitors busy all year round.

If it's elegance, style, and sophistication you want, look no further than Milan. For all of the above, but with an ancient Roman relic seemingly on every street corner, try Rome. For romance – and to fire even the most dormant of imaginations – is there anywhere more suitable than La Serenissima (Venice)? For pizza, try its birthplace, the pulsating southern city of Naples. For gelati, it's got to be Sicily. For art and architecture, it must be Florence – the jewel in the Tuscan crown – and the best place to soak up and revel in the incredible contribution of Italian artists to world culture.

When the traveler tires of historic cities, shimmering coastlines, fashion meccas, and artistic goldmines, there's always exploration of the see-what-happens variety. Meanderings through hilltop villages with cobbled streets, stone houses, fine produce, local wines, and amiable locals will never disappoint. This is *la dolce vita*, after all.

#The North

The Italy of many a traveler's imagination, the northern part of the country boasts natural and man-made marvels on a jaw-dropping scale.

The city of Milan sums up the style, wealth, and cultural depth of the region, while other cities such as Venice and Verona ooze with the tradition, iconography, and visual spectacle that is Italy. Art, architecture, and fine cuisine are bountiful in every city, town, and village in the area.

These man-made riches are set against what is surely one of the finest and most geographically diverse landscapes in the world. From alpine mountains and glacial lakes to the sunny shores of the Riviera and Adriatic, this area offers an adventure for all tastes from hiking to snowboarding to good old-fashioned relaxation.

#Milan

The second-largest city in Italy is often associated with the F word. Actually, two of them: Fashion and Finance.

Post-Brexit, some say Milan is the "new London." It has the largest economy among European non-capital cities and is the second wealthiest city in the EU.

This bustling, stylish metropolis remains Destination Central for Italian fashion and film stars. Supermodels and paparazzi descend on the city twice a year for the fashion shows. High streets and covered arcades brim with expensive, elegant shops.

Fashion and finance aside, Milan's got some history. Its cathedral, the Duomo, took five centuries to complete and is the fourth largest church in the world. Work was started in 1386 and was completed in 1805 by Napoleon Bonaparte.

#madonnina

Symbol of the city and patroness of the Milanese people, the Madonnina was raised onto the main spire of *the Duomo di Milano*, Milan's magnificent Gothic cathedral, in December 1774. The huge statue, composed of embossed and gilded copper plates, stands 14ft tall.

#sevenstars

Opened in 1877, the famed Galleria Vittorio Emanuele II (named after the first king of Italy) is a magnificent four-story shopping arcade with luxe retailers like Prada, Massimo Dutti, Gucci, and Louis Vuitton as well as the world's only seven-star hotel. The glass and iron roof roof reaches a height of 154 ft.

#fashioncapitaloftheworld

Renowned and emerging designers present their collections at Milan Fashion Week, held biannually each year since 1958. Shows take place in historic areas like Milan's central square, Piazza Duomo, which dates back to the 14th century, as well as in showrooms and studios, or just on the city's cobblestoned streets.

#navigliograndecanal

Boasting galleries, bike paths, bars, and boutiques, the funky neighborhood of Navigli dates all the way back to 1179, when its waterways were constructed to connect Milan to the nearby lakes, largely for the purposes of transporting precious Candoglia marble used to construct the city's cathedral.

Lake Como is the deepest lake in Italy. It's known for its unusual shape, like an upside down Y, and the shoreline is dotted with villages and villas, some converted into luxury hotels.

#Lake Como

With its spectacular coast, picture-perfect villages and glorious sunshine, it's no surprise that Lake Como has been drawing in the A-list crowd for decades. This 56 sq mile jewel in the crown of northern Italy has been a summer hotspot for visitors since ancient Roman times. More recently, stars including George Clooney, Madonna, and Richard Branson have all owned homes here, while an influx of other celebs can be found enjoying annual vacations.

One of the best ways to see Como is by hire boat, from which the stunning scenery can be viewed, and any number of charming little towns await for a stop-off to visit historic churches, tour grand villas, or have lunch.

#luxelife

The legendary historic villas of Lake Como provide an opportunity to step back in time and experience life as the wealthy European families, acclaimed novelists, artists, and composers who once lived here did, inspired by the charm and serenity of this magical place.

#romance

Love and money go together like horse and carriage at this wedding location of choice for the rich and famous. One of the most prestigious billionaire weddings of all time happened here when Spotify CEO Daniel Ek got hitched: Chris Rock officiated with Mark Zuckerberg in support and Bruno Mars on stage.

Charting a luxury liner from Portofino can cost hundreds of thousands of dollars a week – or you can enjoy a ringside view from a cafe on the harbor.

#Portofino

Portofino's the place to steal a slice of *la dolce vita*. This little fishing village on the Italian Riviera coastline boasts high-end boutiques, gift shops, art galleries, and seafood restaurants fringing its historic Piazzetta, a small cobbled square overlooking the harbor.

Both in the town and perching precariously up in the cliffs and hills surrounding it are the quaint pastel-colored houses that are this town's signature. A path leads from the Piazzetta to Castello Brown, an historic fortress and museum with art exhibitions and panoramic views of town and the Ligurian Sea.

The small bay is filled with immaculately painted fishing boats, bobbing in sync with slick luxury cruises and yachts. Crystal clear water shimmers all around.

Buone vacanze!

#superyachts

The little fishing village of Portofino is now known as the yachting capital of the Italian Riviera, and some say it's the most photographed port in the world. Yacht berths in the center of town are few and far between, which is a good excuse to take to the sparkling turquoise waters surrounding it.

#viewsviewsviews

Improbable clifftop homes dot the cove just out of the harbor from Portofino. Gazing upwards from the water's edge, the surrounding hillsides are covered with lush green cypresses. It's steep at times, but worth the effort to hike up to Castello Brown, Portofino's 16th-century fortress, for spectacular views.

Langkofel, one of the mightiest of the Dolomites' mountains, at sunset.

#The Dolomites

The Dolomites are strange, jagged pinnacles that jut up like the edge of a steak knife. Eighteen peaks span a range of 350,000 acres. Art buffs might even recognize them as the mountain range in the background of Leonardo di Vinci's *Mona Lisa*.

Below the mountain peaks, rivers meander through valleys dotted with peaceful villages, while pristine lakes are overlooked by fairy-tale castles.

In spite of the beauty of this region, the expansive mountain ranges of northeastern Italy have remained relatively undeveloped. To those in the know, however, the Dolomites offer some of the world's greatest hiking and skiing opportunities.

#sellaronda

Not for the faint-hearted nor the inexperienced, the famous Sellaronda, a circular ski route leading round the mighty Sella massif, offers 25 miles of downhill trails that can be raced in a single day. To ski along the entire Sellaronda takes about six hours, including descents, ascents, and breaks.

#apresski

After a challenging day on the slopes, a steady stream of skiers pours into Selva each afternoon, giving the little town a merry vibe. Others get their party on at one of the après-ski clubs of Val Gardena, where good company, great cocktails, and pumping tunes are the order of the eve.

The emerald-green waters of
Pragser Wildsee (Lake Braies) in
the Dolomites, a Unesco World
Heritage Site.

#Pragser Wildsee

When you finally catch a glimpse of Pragser Wildsee (also known as Lake Braies) your breath is guaranteed to be taken away. Luminous turquoise waters are enclosed by dark green forests themselves engulfed by the bare rock faces of the surrounding mountains. Mountain plateaus are dotted with traditional Alpine huts.

Pragser Wildsee, the so-called Pearl of the Dolomites, changes character dramatically by season. The bright blue summer skies give way to the golden colors of fall which fade into the blanketing ice and snow of winter.

A modern-day Juliet admires the view across the city of Verona.

#Verona

Bathed in the dusky pink glow of sunset, the terracotta roofs, domes, and spires of Verona, nestling adjacent to the fulsome Adige River, look an impossibly romantic prospect. And this is, of course, the most romantic city in the world, best known for its Shakespearean associations as home to Romeo and Juliet.

Beyond its notoriously star-crossed lovers, Verona is a hustling, bustling city, dominated by a vast and extremely well-preserved first-century amphitheater, the venue for the city's not-to-be-missed annual summer opera festival.

Add to that some historic churches, wondrous bridges, first-rate art galleries, and bountiful regional produce and Verona is a place to inspire and enjoy.

#operaplease

Arena di Verona, the third-largest Roman amphitheater, was built in the first century AD by the Flavian emperors. For almost 400 years gladiators fought here entertaining the masses with bloody carnage. Opera is more a common form of entertainment these days and you are usually sure of a seat in the 22,000-seat arena.

#dinnerfortwo

Tucked away in the narrow backstreets of Verona are a host of traditional *osterie* serving simple fare, or trattorias perfect for a traditional dinner. When in Verona try the risotto, a popular dish here. The city also has Michelin-starred restaurants for a different experience.

#handsoff

Juliet's house (Casa di Giulietta) is one of the main attractions of Verona with the most famous balcony in the world. It's said that touching the right breast of the bronze statue of Juliet in the small courtyard will bring luck to all who are trying to find their true love. However, it is causing damage to the statue.

#lovelocks

Couples, families, and friends fasten love padlocks outside the house attached to Juliet's famous balcony. The Capello family once owned this house and are thought to have been the model for the Capulets of *Romeo and Juliet*.

The Grand Canal, Venice's main waterway and "boulevard," is best viewed from one of the many rooftop terraces and restaurants that line its two-mile course.

#Venice

La Serenissima, or the Most Serene One, as Venice is known, is a city-state that has endured more than 1100 years of history.

Built on more than 100 small islands in a lagoon in the Adriatic Sea, Venice has no roads, just canals, including the Grand Canal, which is the equivalent of the main street – one that's lined with Renaissance and Gothic palaces, that is.

The central square, St. Mark's Place, contains St. Mark's Basilica, tiled with Byzantine mosaics, and the Campanile bell tower which presides over the city's red roofs.

Venice is most famous for its fleet of gondolas and gondoliers, who sweep tourists gracefully through the city's waterways, large and small. It is, of course, also known for romance, which is the signature of the city.

#bigloungeroom

The largest square in Venice, St. Mark's Square is a wide slab of flat, open land in a waterborne city. As such, it has long been an important meeting place for Venetians and was once a centerpiece for its aristocratic class. Napoleon is said to have coined it "the drawing room of Europe."

#sobeautiful

This Venetian Gothic palace on St. Mark's Square was the residence of the Doge, the Duke of Venice. First built in the 10th century, then enhanced as the city grew, it was at the heart of official life, and for 400 years controlled trade in the Mediterranean. Today, the Doge's Palace is a major museum of the city.

#bridgeofsighs

Built in 1600 from white limestone, this ornamental footbridge connected the Doge's Palace with the prison, and inmates could be seen being led across it to their cells. Today the Bridge of Sighs is the most romantic spot in a most romantic city; it's said that couples who pass under it while the bells of St. Mark's toll will be united forever.

#gondolas

In the 17th century around 10,000 gondolas weaved through the city. Today, 400 or so ferry tourists about. All gondolas are black (it's the law) and built to the same specs – weight and dimensions are legally mandated – out of eight types of wood. One side is slightly longer than the other to account for the weight of the gondolier.

#mostfamousbridge

Completed in 1591, the famed Rialto Bridge has become one of the great symbols of Venice. Three walkways stretch across the bridge: two along the outer balustrades, and a wider central walkway between two rows of shops that ply wares to passing tourists.

#masksandmasquerades

This small, wealthy city developed a unique culture of mask-wearing to conceal the identity of the wearer who may be doing a business deal or engaged in decadant behavior. The wearing of masks was banned during Austrian rule. Today the celebration of Carnival has reinvigorated the art and craft of Venetian masks.

A working fishing island in the Venetian lagoon, Burano is a popular day trip for tourists.

#Burano

By day, the island of Burano is a multi-colored masterpiece – a real-life canvas that might have been painted by a modern artist. Full of interesting shops – lots of them selling the trademark lace that the island is famous for – Burano also has some of the best and most economical fish restaurants in the city.

There are lots of legends about why the fishermen colored their homes so brightly. One has it that they painted the houses the same color as their boats. If the boat became shipwrecked, and the sailor lost at sea, the color of its hull would indicate which home would be door-knocked. A less dramatic reason may have been to distinguish one home from its neighbor, especially when seen from sea.

A cobblestoned street in Parma.

#Parma

Parma is a university city in Italy's Emilia-Romagna region, catapulted to worldwide fame thanks to Parmesan cheese and Parma ham.

Romanesque buildings, including the frescoed Parma Cathedral and next to it, the medieval Baptistery, fully coated in pink marble from Verona, are notable monuments in the city center.

Classical concerts and opera take place at the Royal Theater, a 19th-century opera house (pictured right). Originally a fairly sober building, a renovation in 1849 bedecked the interior in lush red velvet and golden ornamentation.

The national art gallery in Parma, Galleria Nazionale, housed inside the impressive Palazzo della Pilotta, displays works by painters Correggio and Canaletto.

#handsoffmycheese

In the Middle Ages, monks around Parma started making a distinctive hard cheese. By the 1530's, Italian nobles began to refer to this cheese as Parmesano, meaning "of or from Parma." In 2008, European courts decreed that Parmigiano Reggiano is the only hard cheese that can legally be called Parmesan.

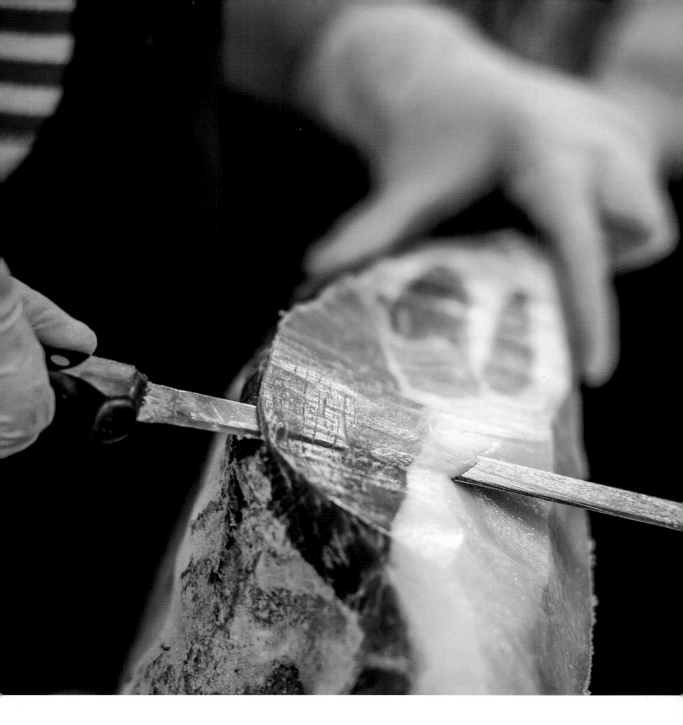

#stampofapproval

It's the real deal. But only if it's made from a particular breed of pig, is salted and cured for up to three years, and passes a strict test. The Prosciutto di Parma Consortium rejects hundreds of thousands of the nine million hams produced each year, which stops them being fire-branded with the official stamp.

Picturesque Manarola is the second-smallest village of the five that make up Cinque Terre.

#Cinque Terre

The crowning glory of the Italian Riviera is the string of five towns (*cinque terre* in Italian) that sits snugly in the habitable nooks at the base of the rugged cliffs that dominate the landscape.

These seaside villages – each one hundreds of years old – feature brightly colored houses with vineyards clinging to steep terraces, harbors bobbing with fishing boats, and trattorias serving seafood freshly plucked from the waters of the Mediterranean.

Once sleepy villages, they are nowadays abuzz with tourists. Only 4000 people live here, but just shy of 2.5 million tourists descend on the towns of Corniglia, Manarola, Monterosso al Mare, Riomaggiore, and Vernazza each year.

The Sentiero Azzurro cliffside hiking trail links the villages and offers walkers sweeping views of the water.

RIGHT **Vernazza is considered by many to be the most beautiful of the five villages that make up this region.**

#walking

Sentiero Azzurro (the Blue Path), the most famous trail in the region, is a 7-mile path connecting the five villages of Cinque Terre. Marked walking paths snake along the mountains that rise behind the towns, passing through terraced vineyards and pine forests with breathtaking views of the coast and sea below.

#chilling

Cinque Terre's namesake wine is a crisp, light-bodied white made primarily from the native grapes Bosco and Albarola. The real jewel of Cinque Terre is the dessert wine, Sciacchetrà. Made with the same blend as Cinque Terre, this rare honeyed nectar is made from the best grapes grown closest to the sea.

#remote

Corniglia is the smallest and the highest town of Cinque Terre. There's no port and access by car is almost impossible, so by train or foot are the only options. From here, a beautiful (nudist) beach, Guvano, can be reached by foot and (adding to the drama) with a torch to navigate the 0.6 mile tunnel en route.

#shimmerandsparkle

The only sandy beach in Cinque Terre makes the popular town of Monterosso al Mare one of the busiest, with the most resort-like vibe of the five towns. It also boasts important historical monuments, plentiful restaurants, and small hotels, as well as the sparkling waters of the Med on its doorstep.

#Central Italy

Central Italy is a region that's rarely skipped on the itinerary mainly thanks to the city of Rome, a non-negotiable for travelers who don't want to miss out on the chance to wander around a modern-day metropolis where ancient monuments pop up randomly on the streets and on the skyline. Here too is the Vatican City, providing a unique insight into the history, traditions, and ceremony of the Catholic religion in Italy.

Beyond Rome, rolling hills, cyprus trees, and hilltop villages are a trademark of central Italy's other highlights – the regions of Tuscany, known as the "crown of Italy," and Umbria. Days, weeks, or as long as you can spare spent exploring hilltop villages, drinking local wines, and indulging in regional produce will be time well spent.

At Tuscany's heart, the achingly beautiful city of Florence provides another opportunity to step back in time and to indulge in Italy's fine artistic heritage at the Uffuzi Gallery.

The trademark cypress trees of Tuscany.

#cityofpuccini

Dating back to Roman times, the stunning city of Lucca boasts medieval and Renaissance churches, towers, piazzas, and one of the best-preserved historic city walls in Europe. Composer Puccini's place of birth has been transformed into a museum, painstakingly restored to how it was when the he lived there.

#towerhouses

At the height of its glory, San Gimignano had 72 fortified tower houses built by the nobility as symbols of their wealth and power. Although only 14 have survived, San Gimignano still retains its feudal atmosphere and appearance.

#cellardoor

Rolling hills covered in grape vines, olive, and cypress trees and dotted with old hilltop castles, this region is the epitome of wine country, boasting some of Italy's most famous appellations. The main wine regions are located less than two hours from Florence or Siena, and can be visited as a day trip.

#chianticlassico

Tuscany is home to Chianti, a traditional red wine made across the region. Legend has it that in 1716 the Grand Duke of Tuscany decreed that this region could produce what is known as Chianti Classico. For wine to be called Chianti Classico, it must consist of at least 80 percent of the local grape variety, Sangiovese.

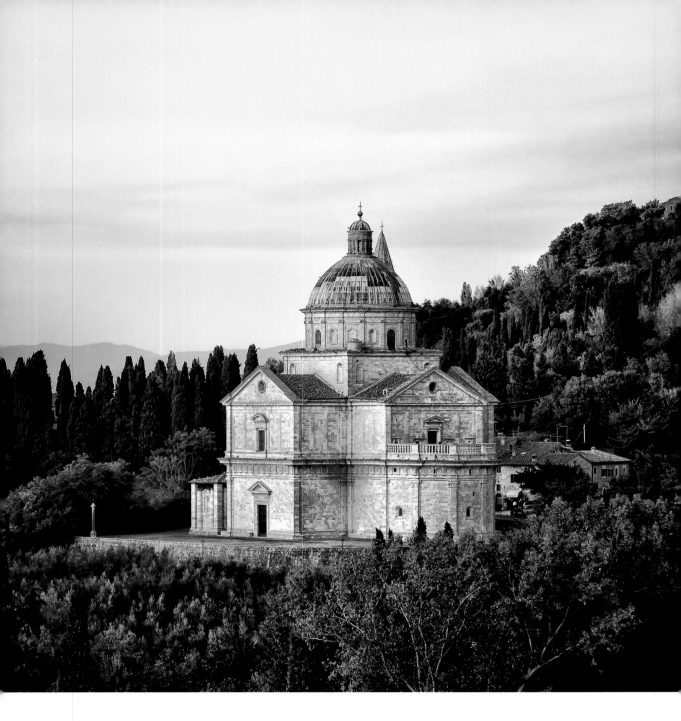

#timestoodstill

The church of San Biagio sits in the valley just below Montepulciano, a city with elegant Renaissance palaces, ancient churches, and one of the most intact and architecturally unified historic centers of any Italian town. Within its walls, no major building work has taken place since 1580.

#fortresstown

Monteriggioni, a medieval, walled town built on a hill by the Sienese in the 13th century as protection against Florentines seeking to expand their territories, is considered one of the best-preserved medieval towns in Italy. It boasts magnificent exterior walls with 14 towers on square bases and town buildings inside.

#popetown

Pienza was the birthplace of Pope Pius II, top dog from 1458 to 1464. It wasn't a lengthy reign but enough to order that his small village be rebuilt as an "ideal city." So it is that this small community of 2000 people now lives in a town boasting a Renaissance cathedral, marble palace, and 40 similarly impressive buildings.

PECORINO
FRESCO
€ 12.80 al Kg

PECC
STRAC
€ 1

PECORINO
SEMIFRESCO
€ 14.80 al Kg

#localproduce

It's not all cathedrals and palaces in Pienza though. This small town punches above its weight in terms of restaurants, cafes, and shops selling local produce. Visiting Pienza provides a window into the stunning and productive Val d'Orcia and the wine and food that comes from this region.

One of many impressive statues at the open-air Piazza della Signoria, that of Perseo holding Medusa's head, by Benvenuto Cellini (1554), is a terrifying reminder of what happened to those who crossed the Medici.

#Florence

It speaks volumes that the entire city center of Florence is a Unesco World Heritage Site. The core of this little city hasn't changed much since the Renaissance. Cobbled streets are regularly interrupted by elegant squares, 16th-century palaces, medieval chapels, and marble basilicas, and open-air sculpture is seemingly around every corner. History, art, and architecture are jam-packed into this small city on the banks of the Arno River. It is a perfect place to soak up the past, indulge in some of the finest Italian art on display anywhere in the world, and feast on gourmet Tuscan cuisine.

#brunelleschi'sdome

The glorious cathedral of Santa Maria del Fiore was built in 1296, but its grand dome did not come until 1436. With his double-shell dome design, architect Filippo Brunelleschi found a solution to the problem of how to erect a dome 150ft wide 180ft above the ground, atop the existing walls.

#28greatmen

The niches beneath the porticos of the Uffizi Gallery were originally designed as architectural features but an enterprising Florentine printer, Vincenzo Batelli, devised a lottery scheme to fund the construction of 28 sculptures of important men of the day. These were popular at a time when civic and city pride ran high.

#secretwalkway

One of the most famous bridges in the world, Ponte Vecchio was built in 1350, after a catastrophic flood in 1333 carried away its predecessor. The private aerial walkway that runs over it was built so the Medici family could move between the seat of government and their private residence, safe from risk of assassination.

#famousbridge

To recoup the cost of the Ponte Vecchio, the government of Florence rented out the 46 shops built on it. Shopkeepers began to alter the structure, and by the 16th century the old battlements had gone and windows had appeared. Today it is famous for wooden-shuttered goldsmiths' shops that line both sides.

#uffizigallery

Initially built in the mid 1500's as offices *(uffizi)* for magistrates, the top floor was turned into a private gallery for the Medici family to enjoy with society of the day. In 1769, it was opened to the public as a museum with 50 rooms, housing paintings spanning five centuries, including works by Giotto, Leonardo, and Michelangelo.

#david

In 1501, Michelangelo received a commission to create a statue of David and Goliath from a large block of marble lying unused within the Duomo Cathedral's workshop. He took just 18 months to create it, working on his own and hidden behind a wooden cage so that no one could see the statue before its unveiling.

At 184ft tall with eight floors and approximately 300 steps, the Leaning Tower of Pisa inclines approximately four degrees, giving the impression of falling.

#Pisa

Once a maritime power akin to Venice, Pisa now draws its fame from an architectural project gone wrong. But the world-famous Leaning Tower is just one of many Romanesque buildings, Gothic churches, and Renaissance piazzas in this captivating city. Pisa's elite university has been attracting students from across Italy since the 1400s, and the presence of so many students gives the center of town a vibrant street life dominated by locals rather than tourists.

The Leaning Tower of Pisa is set in the Piazza del Duomo (Cathedral Square), a walled 21.9-acre area. A Unesco World Heritage Site, the square also contains the Cathedral, Baptistery, and the Monumental Cemetery. In recognition of the extraordinary beauty of the monuments it contains, this palace is popularly refered to as the Square of Miracles.

RIGHT **Interior courtyard of the Monumental Cemetery of Pisa, founded in 1277, and resting place for scores of significant political and intellectual figures, including members of the Medici family and professors from the University of Pisa.**

Siena's Palazzo Pubblico (town hall) began construction in 1297 as the seat of the Republic of Siena's government.

#Siena

A gorgeous medieval piazza, Il Campo, sits at Siena's heart and is the place to see and be seen. Rather than a church, Il Campo gathers around Siena's town hall, a nod to the city's secular tradition.

Perched at the city's highest point and visible for miles around, the white-and-green striped cathedral is as Gothic as it gets. Inside and out, it's dripping with statues and mosaics, and the sculptured eyes of 172 popes peer down on those who enter.

Between the Cathedral and Il Campo are twisting, turning backstreets lined with colorful flags that represent the city's neighborhoods. The rivalry between them is on display during Il Palio, a wild bareback horse race around Il Campo held annually in July and August.

#gothicbeauty

At Siena's heart is Cathedral Santa Maria Assunta, one of Italy's finest Gothic churches, equally stunning inside and out and a showcase for the work of Italy's finest artists of the day: Nicola and Giovanni Pisano, Donatello, Pinturicchio, Lorenzo Ghiberti, and Bernini. The cathedral in its present form was begun in 1229.

#ilcampo

Il Campo (here viewed from the Belltower, Torre del Mangia), is one of Europe's great medieval squares. The red-brick fishbone paving of the piazza is divided into nine segments to represent the Government of Nine, who administered Siena from 1287 to 1355.

Often referred to as the green
heart of Italy, Umbria is a beautiful
and – despite the many visitors –
largely unspoiled region of rolling
hills, woods, streams, and valleys

#Umbria

This small land-locked region with no major cities has got a few things going for it. The scenery for one. Magical pastoral scenes dominate the region – rolling hills with an impossible-to-miss luminous silver haze hanging over them morph into rugged mountains further south. Idyllic hill towns such as Todi or Gubbio serve up perfect medieval architecture, authentic Italian food, and culture without the spit and polish of Tuscany.

Historically, Umbria is known as the birthplace of several saints, St. Benedict and St. Francis of Assisi being the most famous. The town of Assisi and its incredible basilica with extraordinary frescoes by Giotto are a drawcard for tourists.

RIGHT Umbrian town of Trevi at sunset.

#artisticbasilica

The grandiose Basilica of St. Francis might seem an odd memorial to a man who preached abstinence, but it is a global focal point for art and spirituality. The lower church, in Romanesque style, dates from 1230, and the upper one, in Gothic style, from 1253. Great artists of the 13th and 14th century worked on the basilica.

#placeofpilgrimage

Two days after St. Francis's death in 1228 he was canonized, and on that same day, Pope Gregory IX laid the first stone of the future basilica, destined to become the mother house for the Franciscan Order. Assisi's place as the global center of a movement focusing on a message of peace and tolerance was established.

Three thousand years of urban development shows itself in Rome's exhilarating cityscape.

#Rome

Rome is majestic. Its majesty harks back to its days as HQ of the Roman Empire, a gig that lasted a while, from 27 BC until AD 476 in fact. The empire's legacy lives on today with a heady mix of haunting Roman ruins rubbing shoulders with awe-inspiring art and vibrant street life.

Antiquities abound with icons such as the Colosseum, Roman Forum, and Pantheon an easy amble away from most central hotels, while its many ornate piazzas and exuberant fountains add a Baroque touch to the city's captivating streets.

Towering over the skyline, St. Peter's Basilica is the Vatican's showpiece, and a towering masterpiece of Renaissance architecture.

Italy's fiery capital is one of the most famous, romantic, and inspiring cities in the world.

#iconicfountain

Situated at the end of the Aqua Virgo, an aqueduct constructed in 19 BC, the stunning Baroque Trevi Fountain made of travertine stone stands a massive 5ft tall and is almost 65ft wide. With water pumping out of multiple sources, the fountain spills about 2,824,800 cubic ft daily.

#nocrumbsplease

Situated between the former Spanish Embassy and a French church, the Spanish Steps were built in 1723–25 as a symbol of unity between the nations. Fashion house Bulgari recently paid for a major refurbishment to the iconic 135 steps. If it was illegal to eat your sandwiches on them before (it was), then it definitely is now.

#fountains

The most famous and perhaps the most beautiful of Rome's squares, Piazza Navona displays the genius of Bernini, Boromini, and Giacomo della Porta in its three amazing fountains: the Fountain of the Moor, the Fountain of Neptune, and Bernini's masterpiece, the Fountain of the Four Rivers.

#piazzanavona

Lined with Renaissance and Baroque buildings, the breathtaking Piazza Navona, commissioned by Pope Innocent X for his family, is now one of Rome's liveliest places, full of tourists, portrait painters, vendors, musicians, mime artists, shops, and restaurants.

#shoptillyoudrop

The world-famous Via dei Condotti is a designer shoppers' paradise. The street has been at the center of Italian fashion since at least 1905 when Bulgari opened here. Today Armani, Hermès, Cartier, Louis Vuitton, Fendi, Gucci, Prada, Dolce & Gabbana, and Salvatore Ferragamo all have boutiques here.

#gourmet

Food and wine is a serious business in Rome. While there are pizzerias and trattorias on every street corner, it's worth seeking out the new wave of places in Rome that take the fresh-and-local trattoria formula and give it a cordon bleu twist.

#variedpast

The central square of Campo de' Fiori has been a bustling focal point of city life since at least the Middle Ages. After it was paved in the 15th century it became a theater for public executions as well as a hub for travelers who came to stay in the many hotels lining the square.

#traditionaldelivery

In the 19th century Campo de' Fiori became host to one of Rome's most impressive fish and produce markets. To this day every morning the square sees a riot of fresh food trucked in from the Italian countryside to the delight of locals and visitors alike.

#weddingcake

The Altare della Patria monument was built in honor of Victor Emmanuel, the first king of a unified Italy. Designed by Giuseppe Sacconi in 1885, it was inaugurated in 1911 and completed in 1925. It's been termed *macchina da scrivere* (typewriter) or *torta nuziale* (wedding cake) by less-than-impressed locals.

#angelsbridge

The Ponte Sant'Angelo is mind-bogglingly old: it was built between 133 and 134 AD by Emperor Hadrian to link the left bank of the Tiber with his mausoleum, the monumental and majestic tomb he had commissioned. The bridge is flanked by ten angels standing on tall bases, hence the name "Angels Bridge."

#The Vatican

Vatican City is quite something. It is a city and a state of only 0.17 sq miles, with its own coins, own army, own railway (the world's smallest), and a population of 800 people who consume the most wine per head in the world (there's a lot of Communion happening here).

That aside, there's plenty here to keep visitors busy.

The two must-see sights are St. Peter's Basilica and the Sistine Chapel. Entering St. Peter's Basilica for the first time is unforgettable. The size and opulence of the interior are breathtaking, and wherever the gaze rests it seems there is another priceless masterpiece on display.

The Vatican Palace contains magnificent rooms decorated by the greatest artists of their time, as well as priceless collections in more than a dozen museums.

Restaurants on St. Peter's Square, the Vatican's great focal point, provide the perfect respite.

#theobelisk

The 83ft obelisk was first erected in Egypt around 2500 BC. It was brought to the Julian Forum of Alexandria by Emperor Augustus and stood there until Emperor Caligula had it moved to Rome in AD 37. Moved to its current location in 1586, it took 900 men and 140 horses to pull the obelisk upright.

#colonnade

In 1656, Pope Alexander VII commissioned Gian Lorenzo Bernini to create a square worthy of the majesty of St. Peter's Basilica. Bernini's piazza contains four rows of imposing Doric columns on two sides arranged in a stunning colonnade topped with 140 statues depicting saints, martyrs, popes, and church elders.

#snailstaircase

The Vatican Museums consist of several galleries housing art that the Catholic Church has acquired since 1506. Giuseppe Momo was commissioned by Pope Pius XI to create a central staircase that connected them. His creation is made up of two wrought iron stairways – one going up, one going down – that curve in a double helix.

#can'tquitereach

The *Creation of Adam* on the ceiling of the Sistine Chapel took Michelangelo four years (1508–12) to finish. A sculptor, Michelangelo had never painted frescoes before. He constructed a unique scaffolding system to hold workers and materials that was high enough that Mass could be celebrated below.

#Colosseum

An enduring symbol of ancient Rome, the Colosseum may have a dark and disturbing history, but a visit is both a thrilling and essential component of any trip to the city (as 4 million annual visitors attest).

Emperor Vespasian originally commissioned the amphitheater in AD 72 but his son Titus finished the job after his father's death. Titus celebrated its opening with games that lasted 100 days and nights, and during which 5000 animals died.

The outer walls have three levels of arches and at the base 80 entrance arches allowed the spectators to enter and be seated quickly. Inside, spectator seating was divided into three tiers, while a wooden floor provided the stage under which a network of passageways and cages housed the animals and people who were to perform there.

The Colosseum was abandoned with the fall of the Roman Empire in the 5th century, but it remains center stage in the geography and history of Rome.

#lookinside

Inaugurated in AD 80, the 50,000-seat Colosseum was originally covered by a huge canvas held aloft by masts. Inside, tiered seating encircled an arena that was built over an underground complex (the hypogeum) where animals were caged and stage sets prepared for the gladiatorial battles ahead.

#thegoodolddays

The Colosseum saw four centuries of active use, but by the 6th century AD interest in it diminished until it was essentially used as a place to source building materials (marble and travertine) for Rome's great monuments. Restoration began in the 1990s and continues with support of tourists, business, and government.

The impressive remains of
the Roman Forum.

#Roman Forum

Located in a valley separating the Capitoline and Palatine Hills, the Forum developed from the earliest times as a key political, ritual, commercial, and civic center. The site contains a wealth of temples, statues, columns, and civic buildings.

Some impressive Roman engineering is on display here too. Built on marshland in the 6th century BC, the area was drained by means of the Cloaca Maxima, one of the first sewer systems in the world.

Like many of ancient Rome's great monuments, the Forum fell into disrepair after the fall of the empire until eventually it was used as pastureland and extensively plundered for its stone and marble. During the 20th century excavations on the site began and continue to this day.

RIGHT The Arch of Titus at the Roman Forum is a triumphal arch that commemorates Rome's victory over Jerusalem. It was built after the death of the emperor Titus.

The exterior of the Pantheon.

#Pantheon

The Pantheon, meaning "honor all gods," is a remarkably well-preserved ancient monument. Originally a temple, the current version is a church that was commissioned by Emperor Hadrian around AD 126.

Some 2000 years since its construction, the spectacular design, proportionality (the height of the dome is the same as its diameter), and architectural harmony are a reminder of the greatness of the Roman Empire.

The gigantic dome atop the Pantheon has a diameter of 142ft. It claimed the title of the largest dome in the world for 1300 years, and remains the largest unsupported dome in the world.

At the center of the dome, there is a hole of 26ft diameter, known as the Oculus. It's thought that smoke from sacred fires escaped through the hole. Certainly, it is a clever device for letting in the light to this enormous edifice, and reducing the weight of the dome.

#The South

The "boot" of southern Italy basks in blue skies and sunshine, its Apennine mountain range providing a dramatic canvas for the crystal coastline and its sandy beaches. The Mediterranean climate of southern Italy is an important reason for the region's popularity.

The Amalfi Coast, lapped by the Tyrrhenian Sea, nestles around the base of the never-quite-dormant Vesuvius. Containing a wealth of quaint, hilltop villages, the Amalfi is best navigated via the nail-biting coastal road, Strada Statale 163, an experience all of its own. The jaw-dropping ride boasts shimmering coast on one side and volcanic hillsides and plains dotted with olive groves on the other.

Bustling foodie city Naples and laid-back Baroque Lecce provide two extremes of the present and the past for visitors to the area to enjoy. Birthplace of pizza, Naples is also Italy's third-largest city.

The streets of Naples at dusk.

#Naples

Gritty, anarchic, and tattered around the edges, Naples might not be the picture-postcard Italy many travelers aspire to visit. But Italy's third-largest city is a vibrant, sprawling place, bursting with life, and serving up the country's best pizza, pasta, and coffee, and many of its most celebrated seafood dishes, street snacks, and sweets. The original wood-fired Neopolitan pizza was invented here and there's no better place to eat some.

Naples is home to one of Italy's best archaeological museums: the National Archaeological Museum. And art lovers will enjoy the Museo di Capodimonte – only the Uffizi Gallery in Florence has a larger collection of the works of Italian masters such as Raphael, Michelangelo, and Botticelli.

Naples' southern location means the city is close to both Sicily and Sardinia, the ancient ruins of Pompeii, and the beautiful Amalfi Coast.

#gotanywashing?

Three major east-west streets intersect with *cardini* (laneways) running north-south to form the grid of the ancient Greek and later Roman city of Neopoli. The *cardini* are crammed with little shops, and the characterful architecture is famously flagged with laundry.

#musttry

A scene from *Eat Pray Love* was shot at Pizza da Michele in Naples in which Julia Roberts advocates guilt-free indulgence to her dining partner: "This is pizza margherita in Napoli. It is your moral imperative to eat and enjoy that pizza." Many restaurants will only offer two choices: margherita or marinara.

#homeofpasta

In the 19th century, *macaroni* (the term for all pasta) was considered street food to be eaten with the hands, especially in Naples, where it was kneaded in the open air, then dried on makeshift racks. Different parts of the country later developed speciality pasta. In Naples, it was *puttanesca*, spicy and pungent.

#whitesauce

Classic Neapolitan pasta dishes often include seafood. *Spaghetti con le vongole* is a Neapolitan culinary tradition that is served year round and is one of the most important plates of Cena della Vigilia di Natale, the traditional Neapolitan Christmas Eve dinner. In Naples, the sauce for this dish must be white.

A characterful crumbling
facade at a Procida seaside villa.

#Procida

The Bay of Naples' smallest island is also its best-kept secret. This little fishing island has a lived-in and scruffy (in a good way) vibe, providing an authentic "Italian island life" experience to tourists. Visitors who make the trip here will be rewarded by a choice of quiet beaches, many with hidden tracks down to the crystalline waters.

The architecture here is quaint and romantic in the extreme, and has set the stage for Hollywood movies such as *The Talented Mr. Ripley*, which was filmed here.

When the sun goes down on the sun-bleached streets, the restaurants and trattorias come to life, serving up fresh seafood from local waters and chilled limoncello from the glut of lemons grown here – among many other delicacies.

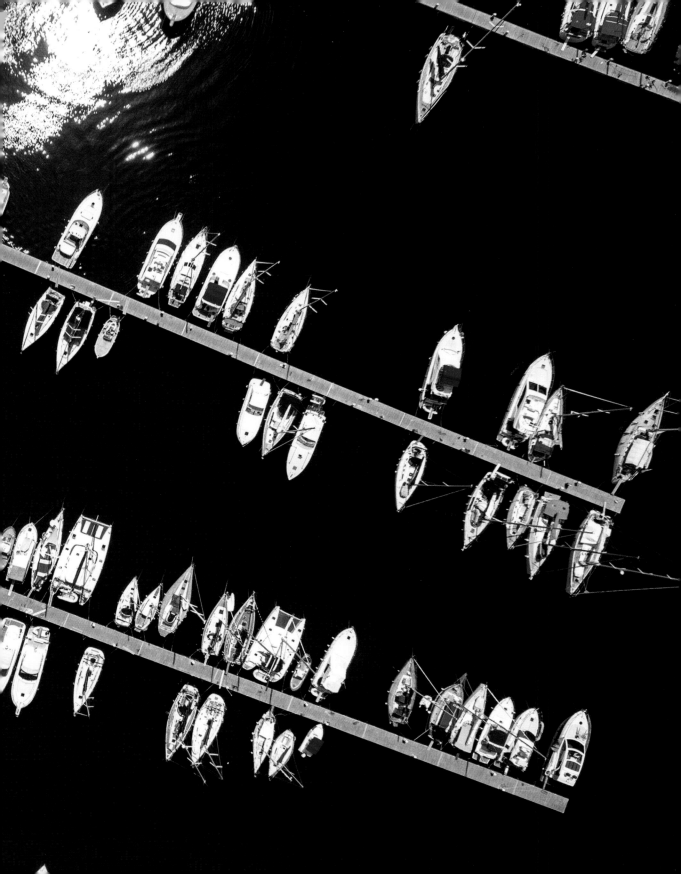

#spontaneous

The harbor of Marina Corricella in Procida is famous for its spontaneous architecture: rows of brightly colored houses seemingly stacked on top of each other form a mishmash of arches, domes, windows, terraces, balconies, and staircases that have provided the backdrop for many a movie set.

#peaceandcalm

The smell of salt air, charming narrow streets, unique architecture, bold colors, and total absence of cars make Corricella a small oasis. Entrance is by stairways and passages hidden among the houses and because of this the village has remained an outpost of peace and calm.

Pompeii is a significant archaeological site that provides an incredible glimpse into the daily life of an average Roman town over 2000 years ago.

#Pompeii

It's hard to overstate the drama of this place. When Vesuvius erupted in AD 79, an entire city was buried under volcanic ash and left undiscovered for 1700 years until archaeologists slowly began to unearth over 2000 bodies that had been frozen in time – walking, sleeping, eating, or talking – as the molten lava stopped them in their tracks.

The volcanic ash also preserved the colorfully frescoed buildings and streets. The result is a unique slice of ancient life, where visitors can walk down Roman streets and poke around in millennia-old houses, temples, shops, cafes, amphitheaters, and even a brothel. Street signs, posters, kitchenware, work tools, and furniture are among the items on display, giving a particularly detailed view of how the Romans lived day to day, in a bustling city.

Luxurious and romantic Positano,
a town famously built into the side
of a cliff.

#Amalfi Coast

Deemed an outstanding example of a Mediterranean landscape by Unesco, the Amalfi Coast is one of Italy's most popular destinations.

The precipitous mountains and sea cliffs are dotted with pastel-colored homes and luxe villas, along with a chorus of fabled towns that are firmly pinned to the travel map. There's jet-set and fashionista favorite Positano, with its chic boutiques and sun-kissed beaches. Further east, ancient Amalfi lures with its historic cathedral.

The region is home to some of Italy's finest hotels and restaurants, cementing its appeal to the A-listers. It's also one of the country's top spots for hiking, with well-marked trails providing the chance to escape the glitterati on the coast.

#almafitown

Amalfi had a glorious history as a maritime republic before much of it slid into the ocean in an earthquake in 1343. The historic Piazza del Duomo in the center of the town features a striking Byzantine-style cathedral with Moorish-influenced arches and decoration.

#roadof1000bends

Famous for its hairpin bends, steep inclines, spectacular ocean views, and terrifying narrowness in parts, the Strada Statale 163 (Amalfi Coast Road) is arguably the world's most stunning and thrilling sightseeing drive. It stretches 30 miles between Sorrento and Amalfi.

#unmistakablypositano

The pastel colors – primrose, pink, terracotta, peach and white – of houses that appear to be stacked effortlessly on top of one another are a key part of the charm of Positano, that sometime playground of the rich and famous and an enduringly popular holiday destination.

#spiaggiagrande

Positano's main beach, Spiaggia Grande, is easily recognizable thanks to the colorful rows of umbrellas and loungers. There's a southern-Italian holiday vibe here, with sunbathers eating pizza on the beach and kids pestering parents for gelato.

#bestlemons

Amalfi and Sicilian lemons are widely regarded by cooks as the most desirable. Such succulent lemons are not waxed, so lemony aromas are immediately released on grating. Grown on the hills in particular around Sorrento and Amalfi these lemons are at their best in the summer months.

#lemonart

The abundant lemons of the Amalfi region are picked fresh to make limoncello liqueur and used extensively in local dishes. The lemon motif provides inspiration for artists in regional ceramics and a citrus scent fills the streets here.

The famous Via Krupp, built by the German armaments manufacturer Krupp, snakes down from the Augustus Gardens to Marina Piccola on the island of Capri. The road is often closed due to falling rocks but the brave (and foolhardy) don't let that stop them.

#Capri

The beauty and decadance of Capri has charmed folk from ancient times to today: Roman rulers and Hollywood legends alike. And here's why. It contains the perfect mix of desirable Mediterranean elements: Roman ruins, glittering seas, gourmet food, high style, and hidden beaches and coves.

Surrounded by the Bay of Naples and Tyrrhenian Sea, the island of Capri lies some 17 miles off the Amalfi Coast. Its 4 sq miles contain townships that includes bustling Capri Town with its high-end hotels, and the more serene Anacapri, in the west, which is popular with hikers.

Capri is mountainous – at 1932ft, Monte Solaro is its highest peak – providing ample opportunity for beautiful terraced gardens and gorgeous panoramic vistas. Sigh.

#Sicily

Goethe famously said "To have seen Italy without having seen Sicily is not to have seen Italy at all." The old master might be long gone but his words remain to inspire and instruct us not to miss out.

The Mediterranean's largest island is culturally distinct and yet somehow seems to encapsulate the essence of the mainland. Historically, it's truly ancient and boasts some of the finest surviving Doric temples and theaters of the ancient Greek world. Culturally, it's unique, with its own brand of the Italian language and distinctive artistic, musical, culinary, and architectural scenes.

But this lush island also boasts some of the best of what visitors expect from Italy: hilltop villages, ancient temples, crystalline waters, endless beaches, fine seafood, pasta and pizza, great wines, and an all-round good time for the lucky tourist.

#harvest

The olive harvest in Sicily takes place between the middle of September and the end of November, depending on the altitude at which the olives are grown. Most major producers harvest the olives by hand and there is a growing number of organic oils being produced on the island.

#thegoodstuff

Sicily produces about 10 percent of Italy's olive oil. There are six DOP (Protected Designation of Origin) olive-oil-producing areas of Sicily, more than in any other region of Italy: Val di Mazara DOP, Valdemone DOP, Valle del Belice DOP, Valli Trapanesi DOP, Monte Etna DOP, and Monti Iblei DOP.

The church of San Giuseppe in Taormina
was built in in the Baroque style between
the late 1600's and the early 1700's.

#Taormina

Taormina sits up high on the cliffs, with beautiful beaches stretching out below. One of Sicily's premier summer destinations, this chic resort town is popular with those wanting a taste of *la dolce vita*.

In the 18th to the mid-20th centuries, the town was a must-see destination on the classic Grand Tour circuit, with notable personalities and royals of the day, such as D.H. Lawrence, Oscar Wilde, Tsar Nicholas II, Elizabeth Taylor, and Greta Garbo enjoying its charms.

Built in the Hellenistic period (3rd century BC) by carving into the hilltop, the Teatro Antico is the second-largest classical theater in Sicily (after that of Syracuse). It was enlarged by the Romans who used it for their gladiatorial games. The well-preserved theater is perched atop steep cliffs plunging 820ft down to the Ionian Sea, with panoramic views of Mount Etna and, even further north, the Calabrian Mountains. Due to its size and acoustics, it is still used to host classical concerts and rock gigs.

#bestgranita

It's said that in ancient Greek or Roman times foot runners brought snow from Mount Etna to Taormina to be flavored with nuts, berries, and honey, and served to wealthy aristocrats. In the 9th century Arabs introduced sugar cane to replace honey. Granita can be eaten for breakfast (coffee), lunch, or dinner here.

#divine

Originating in Sicily, the cannoli was specifically made for Carnivale, with its masquerades and parades, which occurs right before Lent. The crispy wafer tubes are filled with a mildly sweet, creamy ricotta filling that is full of flavor and a staple of Sicilian cuisine.

The Church of San Matteo is located in the heart of Palermo.

#Palermo

It's not a city for the faint of heart. It's brash, loud, dirty (sometimes), and an all-round wild ride most of the time. But if that sounds like your vibe, then saddle up for all that Palermo has to offer.

The essential sights are a mind-boggling display of opulent Norman and Baroque churches and pre-eminent museums of art and archaeology. The impressive Royal Palace of Palermo, once the seat of the kings of Sicily during the Norman domination, is today home to the regional parliament of Sicily.

But an everyday walk through this city, which has existed at the edge of Europe for millennia, will reveal just as much. Spicy, souk-like markets rub shoulders with Gothic palaces, Byzantine mosaics and Arabian marble domes; the scent of lemons fills quiet squares just off fume-filled and manic main streets; and graffiti sprawls across crumbling ancient walls. The historic center is second only to Rome in terms of its size, so start there and see where your itchy feet take you. Just don't forget to look left, look right for the traffic.

When it's time for a sit-down, head to Teatro Massimo, for an authentic Italian operatic performance, or find a local puppet show.

#crowningglory

Completed in 1153, the Byzantine-style church (with a Norman tower) of Santa Maria dell Ammiraglio is glorious inside and out. Glittering and remarkably well-preserved mosaics gild the interior. It was here that Sicily's noblemen convened to offer the crown to Peter of Aragon.

#quattrocanti

Four areas of the old town center meet here at Quattro Canti. The sculptures in the niches on each of the four corners were commissioned by the Spanish viceroy in 1611 and depict a variety of themes, including the four seasons, four Spanish kings, and the four patron saints of the old town areas.

#everydayjokers

Sicilian playing cards date from medieval times and supposedly were introduced by the Arabs. They come in a pack of 42, with 10 cards in each of the four suits. The suits are coins, cups, cudgels, and swords. Each night, groups of men sit together to talk, drink, and play cards in the mild evenings.

#nightlights

Some great cities look almost as good at night as they do during the day, and Palermo is one of them. The civic administration has made a serious effort to promote the city in every way, and flattering lighting is a good example. Christmastime in Palermo takes this to a new level, with its elaborate lighting displays.

Stromboli is perhaps the most
dramatic of the Aeolian Islands. Its
namesake volcano has been erupting
continuously for the last 2000 years,
sending molten lava and crater rocks
spewing into the sky on a regular basis

#Sardinia

Best known for the glitz and glamour of Costa Smeralda, the island of Sardinia has something to offer for the more humble visitor too. Every coast of this magnificent island boats endless white beaches and pristine swimming spots to choose from, and there's fabulous fresh seafood and other culinary joys on offer all over the island too.

Inland, granite mountains provide a rugged backdrop for your travel photos, which would be further enhanced by stumbling upon one of thousands of nuraghi – mysterious Bronze Age stone ruins shaped like beehives – that dot the landscape here. Sardinia's ancient nuraghic culture is unique to the island. Not unique but still amazing is the scattering of Carthaginian and Roman ruins, Pisan churches and Spanish Baroque churches that make a casual appearance here and there on the island.

#costaparadiso

Inlets boasting sandy beaches dotted for 5 miles along the Costa Paradiso from Monte Tinnari to Punta Cruzitta are a delight to discover. Some have natural swimming pools while others are characterized by dramatic granite rocks shaped by the sand. Pink granite cliffs frame this spectacular coastline.

#bosa

The medieval village of Bosa in the north of Sardinia is considered one of the most beautiful in all of Italy. Brighly colored houses with wrought-iron balconies fronting the water and snaking up narrow alleys are a feature of this ancient town. The busy resort is set on a wide beach overlooked by a 16th-century castle.

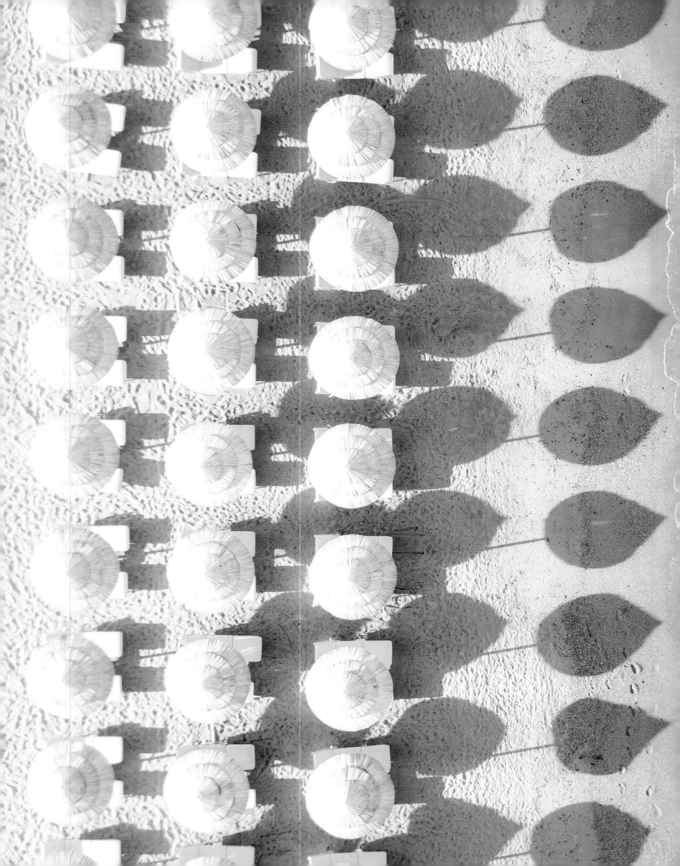

#Costa Smeralda

A magic mix of sun, sea, and luxury defines this exclusive holiday destination.

Dreamy beaches with endless pristine sands, isolated coves and inlets, translucent opal seas, and pink granite rocks are nature's contribution to this spectacular destination. Man has made his mark too, with the development of high-end villas, golf courses, fashionable nightspots, intimate restaurants, the luxury bars and shops of Porto Cervo, and mooring spots for yachts and sailboats.

There are history, culture, and ancient traditions here too, sure, but they take a backseat to the glitz, glamour, and relentless pursuit of the perfect relaxing holiday.

#snorkellinganyone?

The beaches of Costa Smeralda (the Emerald Coast) are characterized by fine, white sand and transparent, emerald-green water, set against a frame of pink granite rocks that have been sculptured by the wind, and lush Mediterranean scrub. The family-friendly Capriccioli Beach is sheltered from the wind.

#luxury

In July and August Porto Cervo's square, boutiques, and yachts and sailing boats host celebrities and VIPs, filling the air with summer gossip. The harbor is considered the centerpiece of the Emerald Coast, with its five-star resorts and hotels, designer shops, upscale restaurants, and exclusive nightclubs.

#Cagliari

Sardinia's capital city is known for hilltop Il Castello, a medieval walled quarter situated high above the town. Highlights within this quarter include the 13th-century Cagliari Cathedral. Viewed from the sea, the city rises helter-skelter in a craze of colors that stretch all the way up to Il Castello.

Behind the scenes, Vespas buzz down palm-lined boulevards and locals hang out at busy cafes tucked under arcades in the seafront district.

As in most Italian cities, ancient Roman ruins, museums filled with prehistoric artifacts, historic churches, and elegant *palazzi* are just a backward glance away.

#littlebundles

Culurgiones are traditional Sardinian stuffed dough pockets whose name means "little bundles," which accurately describes these delicious morsels. They are essentially a delicious soft pasta filled with potatoes, pecorino, garlic, and mint and braided to create a delicate and pretty shape.

#nougat

Nougat is a Sardianian speciality. Egg whites, honey, and almonds produce its characteristic soft texture and ivory color modified by the addition of citrus fruits and spices. Traditionally, Sardinian women were in charge of nougat-making. They would melt honey in a copper cauldron while stirring it with a stick.

HERRON
book distributors PTY LTD

First Published in 2018 by Herron Book Distributors Pty Ltd
14 Manton St
Morningside
QLD 4170
www.herronbooks.com

WWW.CAPTAINHONEY.COM.AU

Custom book production by Captain Honey Pty Ltd
12 Station Street
Bangalow
NSW 2479
www.captainhoney.com.au

This edition first published in 2019.

Cataloguing-in-Publication. A catalogue record for this book is available from the National Library of Australia

ISBN 978-0-947163-19-8

Printed and bound in China by Shenzhen Jinhao Color Printing Co., Ltd

1 2 3 4 5 6 7 8 9 10

PHOTO CREDITS

Front cover: Andreas Zerndl
Back cover: Anton Ivanov

All images used under license from Shutterstock.com
except for pages: 2, 8, 10, 16, 20, 33, 38, 50, 53, 70, 100, 104, 130, 216 © Unsplash